THE FOUR KEYS

A Simple Guide to Authentic Acting

Also by the Author

THE FOUR PRINCIPLES: Applying the Four Keys of
Authentic Acting to Life available on Amazon and
www.EKatherineKerr.com

JUNO'S SWANS, a comedy about sisters available on
Amazon and through Dramatist Play Service

I was in a production of *Urban Blight* with E. Katherine Kerr at the Manhattan Theatre Club. I always stayed in the wings and watched riveted every night. At the end of a scene, she was totally alone—a judgmental, bitter, emotionless woman facing the death of her son. It seemed as if she was going to let go of him and a balloon without feeling anything, but I knew better. I wouldn't have missed this moment for anything. Saying nothing, Katherine let the balloon go, but just before it flew away, she grabbed the string with a heart wrenching sob, and pulled it back to her body as if it were her son—her baby.

Being a musical theatre gal myself, it was one of the most powerful moments I had ever seen onstage, and yet it was never quite the same. Always deeply affecting, her emotion seemed to burst forth fresh and different every night while being always real and truthful. I knew I was in the presence of someone who held the answers. I thought, "Somewhere I have the ability to do that. I want to know how."

When I asked her how she did that night after night, she told me about her Creative Explosion Workshop; a weekend of intense training, exercises, and information applying her Four Principles to acting and to life. I quickly enrolled. It was in that powerful workshop that I finally found out how to be fully present onstage. My eight shows a week have never been the same. While the workshop had an enormous effect on my acting, unexpectedly, it also touched me more deeply. It was life changing.

Faith Prince, Tony Award Winning Actress and Singer

Last night I audited your class. It was the first acting class I've ever attended where there wasn't any acting going on. I left without saying anything to you. I began to weep as I walked 42nd Street. I suddenly realized it was all right. That I was all right. That I was enough.

—*Mark Ransom, actor, poet, singer, songwriter*

Finally, a process that gets you out of your head and into the core of your individual uniqueness as an actor as well as a human being.

—*Jerry Pacific, actor*

Talk about a hot seller - Wow! Personally I think it's your duty to put them on the bookshelves as they *are* what is needed in this field. Your inspiration is more than helpful. It's inspiring. It's brave. NEVER have I EVER been so willing to let go and have faith, be courageous, daring, open, giving, and willing to share myself, until I started on this journey. You have opened up my eyes not only as a performer, but as a writer, as a person. You've exposed me to me. And overall, I feel whole again. You've brought me back to the beginning…to a place I once was a very long time ago when I was young.

—*Richard Luciano, actor/writer*

I haven't seen you in a long time, but I don't think a day goes by that the gifts—many, many gifts that I have gotten from your classes—don't help me live the way I want to. The Tao, Stephen Mitchell's translation, is a great reassurance that what I learned in E. Katherine Kerr's class is the real deal!

—*Aileen Pare, actor*

I just wanted to let you know that I received some good news recently. I won a huge screenplay contest called the Chesterfield Film Writer's Program. I won $20,000. I wanted to thank you because I really believe you had a major part to play in this happening to me because of your support/belief in me, and I wanted to thank you for that and for everything you've done for me. I really mean that.

—*Greg Gasawski, actor/writer*

I am sitting here in the peace and quiet of a Saturday morning and doing my gratitude journal. And your class and what it is allowing me to feel is now frequently on my list. I just wanted to take the opportunity to tell you how your class is changing my life. I have been crying and "feeling" more than I have in years. I feel alive and not like I am just going through the motions.

—*Dana Hubbe, actor*

I'm still in the euphoria of this inspirational-lifting-up experience in the sanctuary of your beautiful home. I'm exhausted, in a good way—finding a way to use that emotion is brilliant—to embrace it, not run from it. And you provided a very safe haven for all that to happen. And weren't there fascinating and uplifting moments from everyone?

—*Jo Anne Parady, actor, director*

As an actress Katherine is captivating, with a presence that dynamically changes a room from the moment she enters. That presence, which comes from her courageous ability to live utterly in the moment, is what she brings to teaching and what she teaches. The principles of acting I encountered in Katherine Kerr's class and my subsequent experience in her Creative Explosion workshop continue to teach and inspire me as an actor, director and educator.

I invited her to speak at a symposium here at Hofstra University. Well over a hundred people were present for the symposium and Katherine, alone on stage, easily engaged the entire room with stories of her experiences. During the question and answer period, a student actress in the front row asked how she could address staying present and fully committed during performance. Katherine's focus on the student was so powerful it suddenly seemed as if there was no one in the room but those two. My students are still talking about her visit last fall, and I hope to have her return as soon as possible. I can both enthusiastically and without reservation recommend her work.

—Jean Dobie Giebel, Associate Professor Department of Drama and Dance, Hofstra University

THE FOUR KEYS

A Simple Guide to Authentic Acting

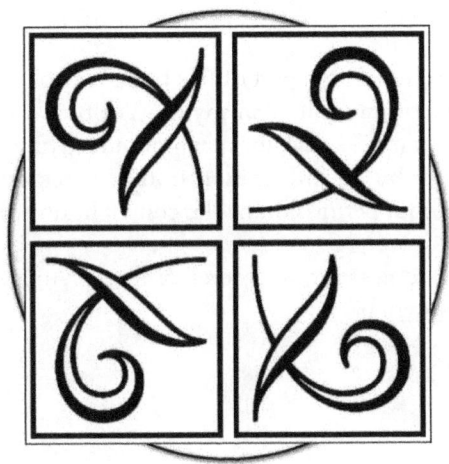

E. Katherine Kerr

CONTENTS

FOREWORD

I've known Katherine since I saw her perform Off-Broadway in Caryl Churchill's play *Cloud 9*. I was so excited and moved by her performance (and by the play) that I saw the production three times. Sometime after that I directed Katherine in a play at the Young Playwrights Festival, and she and I became friends.

As I was writing my play *Laughing Wild*, which has a very demanding leading female role, I began to picture Katherine in the part. And she and I then acted together in the play's premiere off-Broadway at Playwrights Horizons.

Katherine began to teach a course of her own invention called *The Creative Explosion*. For the first weekend, she invited me to be a participant along with five other people, including actress June Havoc.

The weekend consisted of exercises, and the performing of prepared pieces a few times, looking for different perspectives and deeper connections to the material. It was an emotionally and professionally rich workshop, and also one of great bonding among the participants.

Since then, Katherine has continued to teach these workshops, as well as her regular acting classes. I am always running into young actors who, upon realizing I know Katherine, tell me with enormous enthusiasm how much they have benefited from her classes. Sometimes they feel their lives have been changed.

Knowing Katherine as a friend, as an actress, and as a teacher, I would say that she brings the following qualities to all her wit: a sharp intelligence, her own acting abilities (which are substantial), her desire to help and empower people, her sense of humor, her sense of play, a gift for helping people work through artistic and personal blocks, and her inability to settle when she can imagine something better.

Sometimes I long to settle (or to give up, at least for a little while), but I need Katherine to remind me that's not the way to go.

Christopher Durang, Tony Award winning playwright, Co-Chair, Playwriting Program, Juilliard School.

INTRODUCTION

Over the years, the bar has been rising so high in acting that it has become practically an extreme sport. The era of pretending is in the ancient past. We have come a long way from practiced gestures, thick makeup, and putty noses. "Authentic" is the watchword of brilliant acting now.

In order to be truly authentic, actors are taking command of their bodies, minds, and emotions like never before. They lose weight, gain weight, and train like athletes. They explore deep into their emotions like brave spelunkers by means of therapy, yoga, and a myriad of workshops (my own included) that bring to the surface withheld feelings and fears. The ubiquitous Twelve Step programs proliferate where artists gather, perhaps not because more of them are alcoholics and drug addicts than the rest of the world but because more of them are trying *not* to be ruled by addiction and dysfunction.

The notion that an actor needs to be crazy to be brilliant is passé. That does not mean an actor may not start from some kind of trauma in childhood or later. Most actors I know do. Creativity is a natural draw for the heart-scarred. And that pain is what makes us uniquely suited to understand a wide range of human suffering.

In the words of Rumi, "The wound is the place where the Light enters you." And acting, like any form of creativity, is a miraculous way to alchemize the lead of pain into inspirational gold.

That said, too many wounded if brilliant actors have ended up drug addicts, with their lives in a mess or, tragically, dead.

On the other hand, actors and creators who commit to healing and inner exploration are better able to withstand the slings and arrows of a career and even the onus of success. Yes, it's difficult for people to believe that achieving fame and money and awards are so hard to accept with ease, but trust me, while failures and disappointments can be devastating; success can be even more challenging. It takes a very healthy person to face that with grace and keep going.

Not coming to acting until my late twenties, I was lucky to have had a career at all. My own deep scars made it natural for me to step into roles like Blanch DuBois in *A Streetcar Named Desire*. Acting gave me a safe place to feel and that alone was healing. At the same time, I dedicated myself to inner work through many different means.

When Christopher Durang sent me his play, *Laughing Wild*, I was both thrilled and terrified. It turned out to be one of those experiences that make suffering all the slings and arrows of this outrageous career worth it. Being nominated for a Drama Desk Award was the icing on an already delicious cake. But as a side effect, being in this play changed my life in an unexpected and meaningful way.

One night after a performance, I was asked if I would consider teaching an acting class in The Playwright's Horizons theater school.

At first, I demurred. "Oh, thanks, but I don't actually have a technique that I could teach." In fact, when people complimented me on my 'technique' I used to cringe. I didn't have one. "That's okay," I was told. "They'll learn from just being with you."

Disarmed, I said, "Well, let me think about it." In a way, it was as if my life were coming full circle. Twenty five years earlier, after my first year teaching high school English in Indianapolis, Indiana, I had been asked by Mr. Blough, the head of the English Department, to take over for the drama teacher who was retiring the following year.

I was appalled. "I've only been in six plays, and I didn't study acting!! I don't know anything about it!"

He laughed. "Mrs. Beedlemeister has been teaching from pictures in books for the last 35 years. You'll be fine."

So I said to him. "Why don't I go to New York and study acting and then come back and teach?" I'd already been at Indiana University for six years. Why not go to the Mecca of theater to learn acting?

"You'll never come back," he predicted.

"Oh yes I will!" I had no intention of becoming an actress.

And so I came to New York and studied acting at the Neighborhood Playhouse. And then I got cast in an Off Broadway play that turned into a two-year gig. And then…..Well, as it turned out, prescient Mr. Blough was right. I never got back to Indiana.

Now, after all those years, I was being asked again to teach acting, but this time at a professional theater school in New York. Having had so much experience on the stage and in TV and movies, I decided that maybe by now I might have something to offer students. So I accepted the position. And when I finally began teaching acting, everything I had learned in acting and life merged into the Four Keys.

Before meeting with my first class, I tried to remember what I had studied at the Neighborhood Playhouse, but all I could conjure was a "mirroring" exercise in which my partner and I screamed "Fuck you" to one another over and over until we exhausted ourselves.

I considered rushing out to buy books on acting by Michael Chekov and Stanislavsky and read them quickly. I quelled that urge. "Wait a minute." I said to myself. "You haven't used any particular technique in the last twenty-five years. They said being with you would be enough. Go with an open mind and an open heart."

So I did. The only decision I made was to do my best to teach the same way the directors I had worked with had directed me—brilliant, unpretentious, and compassionate directors like Mike Nichols, Tommy Tune, June Havoc, and Ron Lagomarsino for example. They created such a space of trust and respect and relaxation that it brought out the best in actors. They treated me as an equal—a fellow actor—which all of them were. So I determined to give my students this same kind of respect and trust. I vowed never to allow my ego to fall into the godlike stance that I had known other acting teachers adopt.

When I showed up for the first class, the Four Keys seemed to be waiting for me. They announced themselves right from the beginning without fanfare—appearing in full bloom—becoming the basis for this unique acting process. It was as if teaching opened my eyes so that I could see what had been there all along—more of an "oh" than an "aha" moment. My understanding and belief in the value of these keys have deepened, but the keys themselves have not changed from that first eye-opening class.

I found that if I could lead a student to Commit, Be Present, Relax, and Communicate, the results were wonderful and often astonishing. As a result, teaching acting became as joyful and thrilling to me as my own acting experiences.

I have acquired a few questions and techniques that help students fulfill these Four Keys which I am passing on in this short book for you actors, singers and even writers and directors. The keys apply both to you and to the characters you create. I also include a few of my own personal experiences which I hope will illuminate by example.

My wish is that you will take away something from this book that will expand your ability to express yourself as a creator.

January 2015
E. Katherine Kerr

COMMIT

"It's all about love or its opposite."
--Michael Shurtleff

When you read a play or a script, sometimes you become committed to a character immediately. It's like falling in love at first sight—across a crowded room—instantly. You read the script and you know you want to play that part. You can't wait to start rehearsal. It is instinctive. You understand this person in your gut. You recognize them even if they are nothing like you. You fully commit to them before you begin.

Then through rehearsal and performance, you get to know the character more intimately. As in love, it is through being with them that you learn who they are—not through analyzing them before you even know them. If you have ever played a role you loved or, for that matter, fallen in love at first sight, you know this experience.

When you are drawn instinctively to characters, you do not have to think about them or analyze them. In fact, analyzing and talking about them may lead you down the wrong path. Many experienced actors I have worked with don't believe in over-thinking their characters. "Learn the lines and show up" is something I have heard in many different variations. Maureen Stapleton, with whom I toured in Neil Simon's *Gingerbread Lady,* disavowed any acting technique. "Learn your lines and say 'em fast. Fast is good. Faster is better" was the advice she gave me about acting. Of course, it helped that Simon wrote the part for her: Maureen *knew* her character, Evy Meara inside out, and she was brilliant.

I felt the same way about the role in *Laughing Wild* that Christopher Durang gave me. When I read it the first time, I just *knew* her. I never once sat down to think about her or analyze her. As actors, we are lucky to get four or five of those roles in a lifetime.

That said, there are times when we are confronting a character and do not feel that wonderful connection. Then we have to do some digging in order to develop our relationship. And sometimes, the roles that are the most challenging and difficult to understand end up being the ones that are most gratifying.

COMMIT

To commit means to take action. In my definition, I include that which drives the action. Therefore, I define "to commit" as "to tell the truth about what one needs, wants, desires, enjoys, loves, and believes in, and then take action." If you know anything about chakras, you'll notice that need, want, desire, enjoyment, love, and belief line up through the body from the gut to the head. Commitment comes from the body.

Find out what your characters' commitments are. What do they need, really need? What do they yearn for? Dig underneath their surface to learn what is driving them.

In order to step into your characters' shoes as actors, you must know what they may not know themselves. They may *think* they know what they need and want, but it could be a mere fantasy that disguises their real need. They may even lie about it to themselves and others. Or they may be unaware or deny or refuse to admit their true commitments.

You as the actor/singer/writer, must know the truth. "What is their intention?" is a sentence I have heard regarding understanding a character. I say find out what they are desperate for, what they want, need, yearn for, and believe in. What or who turns them on? What's fun for them? What do they love? The stronger their desires, the greater their energy for action. What about their commitment looks a little insane or wrong to others? Are they trying to fly to the moon, make their lives better, reach for the stars, get sober, travel through time or space? The clearer you are about a character's commitments, the closer you will be to the heart of that character.

Years ago, when I took a class about auditioning from Michael Shurtleff, I was deeply impressed when he said, "It's all about love or its opposite." Up to that point, as an actress I had sought to adopt the emotions or the objectives of a character. I now knew to look for the driving force underneath. What is the character passionate about? What is the character committed to?

I heard Neil Simon say, "It's all in the wanting." He identifies what his characters want and then writes without a plan. As a creator, he watches them achieve their desires or not as they play it out.

When stepping into a character, find the strongest commitment you can. That is what makes a character powerful and memorable. The character with the strongest commitment, even one they are forced into, is usually the leading character, the protagonist or the antagonist (e.g. Luke Skywalker or Darth Vader) and the one we want to follow to some conclusion.

We are all committed to something: winning, safety, saving something or someone, surviving, finding love, completing something, inventing something, facing the truth, not facing the truth, hiding, getting revenge, pretending, keeping it together. You must find a connection your character's need. You must step into their shoes and walk their path.

Very often they start on one path and end up on another, for example, in *Dallas Buyers Club*, Matthew McConaughey plays AIDS patient Ron Woodroof. At first he is desperate to save his own life. Then he becomes committed to helping other AIDS patients as well. Initially, he seems driven to do it for money. Eventually, his heart opens to a greater commitment to his fellow sufferers over the course of the story.

Shakespeare hands commitment to you on a platter with Richard III's opening speech:

"And therefore, since I cannot prove a lover

To entertain these fair well-spoken days,

I am determinèd to prove a villain."

So, this is not just mere ambition. He's not just a villain for the fun of being a villain, but he *needs* to compensate for the pain of knowing he can never be loved.

If you are playing the lead, it is not difficult to find the commitment. But if all you are saying is "The patient is ready, doctor" on a daytime drama, in order not to feel like an idiot, you have to step into that person's dedicated shoes. (Yeah, that was one of my lines early in my career.)

Finding out what your character truly wants and needs is like peeling away the layers of an onion. On a conscious level, the character wants_____. On a deeper level, they want_____. And on an even deeper level, they want_____.

Is your character in conflict with his or her desires? How does your character's desires conflict or dovetail with the other characters' desires? Does your character face the truth about his or her authentic commitments? When? And how? Is your character's commitment covert or overt?

When it is unclear, that character may be led into difficult and dramatic situations (e.g. Hamlet). Does the character change commitments over the course of the story? When? Why? What obstacles do they create or face as they move toward or away from their commitments?

THE THREE POSITIONS OF COMMITMENT

There are three positions of commitment:
No. I Don't Want.
I am Open.
Yes. I Want.

Often, a commitment of I Want begins with a strong I Don't Want. Scarlett O'Hara screaming to the sky, "As God is my witness, I will never go hungry again!" is a clear No commitment.

Ghandi says no to British Rule in India and no to violent resistance. It is this No that defines his character. No. I Don't Want can be a very powerful and heroic position. Look not only for what a character wants, but also for what they clearly and honestly do not want. An authentic No stops things. A hero's stance may be all No. No to corruption. No to crime. No to violence. No to lies.

Is your character clear about his or her I Don't Want? Are their No's a lie? Are their No's a denial or resistance to what they deeply want and need and believe in? In the movie, *The King's Speech*, the battle that the teacher, played by Geoffrey Rush, is committed to, is getting rid of his student's stammer. As the movie progresses, so does his commitment to his student—to prove to him that underneath the stammer is a man worthy of being King. On the other hand, Colin Firth's King George VI also wants the same thing. The barriers he must face and conquer make him the hero.

What is your character saying No to? Does this No lead to an even stronger Yes?

Less easy to identify in characters is the Open position. However, it is also a very powerful position. A character in the Open position is often the narrator, the wise one, or the observer in a story. These characters have, perhaps, reached a stage of life that is beyond the Yes and No. Their hearts are open. They are wise. They see. And they are important to the story. They are often the catalysts that break through a protagonist's fear/resistance. This character is perhaps beyond personal needs and goals while remaining compassionate and loving and involved. Yoda in *Star Wars*, The Chorus in Shakespeare's *Henry V* is an example of this Open stance. Is your character in this open, observing. and compassionate position?

There are true open positions and false open positions. Not knowing or admitting what you want is the false position. There are characters in literature who have no idea what they want, and life leads them into situations out of their control. In the old film *Marty*, the conversation between the two guys is a classic example. "Whaddya wanna do, Marty?"

"I dunno. Whadda you wanna do?"

"I dunno."

Sometimes characters know what they want but don't know what action to take. Consider Alice in *Alice in Wonderland* lying on the grass next to her cousin. She's bored. She's uninterested in reading because there are no pictures or conversations in the book at hand. She can't get up the energy to make a daisy chain. What she wants is something interesting to happen but doesn't know how to make it happen. Life in the form of a rabbit with a watch leads her down the rabbit hole and into many insane adventures. Is your character one, who. through lack of commitment, finds him or herself falling down a rabbit hole? Then, of course, the commitment becomes an enforced "How do I get out of here?" "What do I do now?"

The Yes position is more obvious. I want! I need! As an actor you must be able to be as passionately committed as your characters are. What is their deepest most passionate commitment? Is it "I want love?" "I want to dance?" "I want_____?" Or. Is it revenge, hatred, greed, or destruction? These can appear to be the commitment, but hatred is volatile and burns itself out. Look for the love that is underneath the hatred that also fuels it—the disappointment, hurt, greed, or betrayal that covers up the love.

How does your character try to fulfill his or her commitment? What actions do they take or not take? Do they go after what they want tooth and nail? Do they wait for others to act? Do they cajole, seduce, lie, betray, falter, bribe, pretend, punish, threaten, intimidate, plead, beg, borrow, steal, charm, extort or use various other tactics and combinations of tactics to get what they want, what they need, and what they love?

Since the leading characters are usually the ones with the highest level of commitment, you have to be able to find that intensity of commitment in yourself if you are aiming for the leading roles. However, no one can give you commitment. It can be inspired, but it cannot be given. It is yours and yours alone.

What are your true commitments? What are you authentic needs? When have you felt desperate for something? When have you needed something you thought you could not live without? When have you yearned for something with all your heart?

What did you do about those things? Give up? Or pursue? Strategize? Lie to yourself or others about them? Pretend it wasn't true? Cover it up? Deny the truth?

Now think about a character that you have/are working on. What is their deepest need? What do they really want? How does that parallel your commitments now or in the past? Write down everything you know about them on the next blank page.

You must be able to access your own passion, belief, needs, sense of play and fun. When you can, you will be able to step into their shoes.

If you are not clear about your character's commitments, use the Keys in the next three chapters as you work on your role. They will unlock the door to your understanding.

BE PRESENT

"Sensation is at the heart of acting."
--Simon Callow

Being present is the key to knowing what your character's authentic needs and desires are. Being present is also the key to knowing your *own* authentic needs and desires.

One of the greatest compliments an actor can receive is "Oh! You were so *present!*" Great actors ooze presence on stage and on the screen. It's a palpable energy that attracts our attention. They seem to radiate an energy that is more intense and attractive than the average person. The question is, is this an inherent quality in some people or can it be acquired? The answer, fortunately, is that presence is something one can acquire. Learning how to be present will not only give you that extra energetic aura, but it will enable you to understand and fully live inside your character. If you want to be a truly authentic actor, you will dedicate yourself to becoming present in your life as well as on stage.

What do I mean by Being Present? Simply, you are present when you are consciously experiencing the sensations in your body. You are here now physically. That may sound simplistic, but the truth is, most of us know

25

what we're thinking—we may even know what we're feeling, but we are not consciously experiencing the sensations in our bodies.

Being Present was not something traditionally taught in acting classes and is difficult to convey in a book. Without actually being with you, communicating how to be present is a challenge. Most students need a great deal of my guidance to teach them how to be present, so the best I can do in a book is explain it, give examples, and hope you are willing to at least attempt it on your own. Because it is so difficult to explain, I will first relate the thorny story of how I learned to Be Present on stage.

By the time I was cast in *Cloud 9* off B'way, I had already been acting for years, had some success, and learned something of "moment by moment" acting. But it was during *Cloud 9* that I found out what it really means to Be Present.

My role included a beautifully-written monologue about learning self-love. It meant a great deal to me. I was always moved to tears by it. During rehearsal, the director, Tommy Tune, kept placing this monologue later and later in the play. Finally (over the objections of the playwright), he put it right at the end. Opening night went very well. Almost every review favorably mentioned my performance of this monologue during which I simply sat on a chair and spoke directly to the audience.

The light spilling off the stage illuminated the people in the audience, so I could see their reactions clearly. I loved the rapt faces, the tears coursing down cheeks, the snapping of purses as women reached for tissues, and the men shifted to reach into back pockets for their own handkerchiefs.

People in the audience began seeking me out afterwards to tell me how much the monologue affected them—even changed their lives. Some people confided that they hadn't understood the play until the monologue.

26

I began to feel an enormous responsibility towards it and the play. Pressured and scared, I lost my connection to the monologue and dried up emotionally. Seeing the audience as well as I could, with each successive performance I noticed that they were no longer moved. Every performance got worse. The audience, unaware that I could see them, began to demonstrate clear signs that they were actually *bored*. Pocketbooks no longer snapped open. And, horror of horrors, people started reading their programs while I was talking!

Oh, god. Here I was in a hit play that was going to run forever, people had read reviews about this fabulous monologue, and I couldn't do it any more! I was appalled. I tried harder and harder to recapture the feeling to no avail. I was in a state. When I knew the monologue was coming, I'd try to think of everything I could to get myself back to the emotions I had felt—back to the emotions I thought I *should* feel in order to do this beautiful monologue justice. Nothing worked. What to do? I was stymied and afraid I was going to have to quit.

Instead, I got the flu. The understudy was not yet ready to go on, but the show of course must, so I dragged myself to the theater and on stage with a temperature around 104 degrees. I was almost delirious. By the end of the play, I didn't give a fig about the monologue or whether the audience was bored or not. I just wanted to get it over with and go home to bed. I didn't even try to do it right, and I couldn't force myself to feel what I didn't feel. I couldn't deny the truth. I sank into the chair saying the words but really just feeling feverish and sweaty and unbearably sick. I gave up *trying*. I just was where I was—so ill that the experience was surreal. I began to notice, to my great surprise, that this audience seemed moved again! They were paying attention to me again! I could see the tears coursing down rapt faces once more. Pocketbooks snapped open. I was frankly stunned. I hadn't done the monologue "right."

27

I made it home, fell into bed, and couldn't get over the fact that my emotions hadn't been at *all* what I thought they should have been, yet the monologue moved the audience. Strange, indeed.

I was still very ill the next night, but decided to try an experiment. "What if I let myself be exactly where I am and just say the words?" It was a private little test. To my surprise, the monologue worked again.

I took on the experiment like a scientist. "I'm going to see what happens if I just let myself feel whatever I feel— and not try to feel what I think I *should* feel." One night I was feeling extremely happy for whatever reason. I was certain that was not going to work, but I let my happiness speak through the monologue, and it was fine.

Lo and behold! Pocketbooks snapped. Tears coursed. No one read programs. It was a deliciously set up experiment given that the audience thought they were invisible and, therefore, felt no compunction to be nice and pretend I was interesting. A scene partner would continue to pretend interest, but these audiences did not lie. They didn't have to. They were totally honest in their reactions. Being Present in this way was not what I had been taught by acting teachers, but it was wondrous to me how well it worked. If I slipped and tried to do the monologue "well"—or feel what I wasn't feeling, it didn't work.

I expanded my experiment. Early in the show I played a character called Mrs. Saunders. The hilarious Jeffrey Jones and I made one entrance from behind the audience. I remember standing there trying to "prepare" —thinking about the scene that was about to happen on stage. I had the sudden thought, "Oh, why don't you just let yourself be here *now* and trust that you'll be there *then*. Why are you trying to be *there* now? Just be here *now* and there *then*."

Simple as the idea was, it was novel to me. It was kind of mind-blowing. I remember relaxing completely and smiling to myself as I looked at the backs of the heads of the audience and heard them laughing about something that was happening on stage. I loved that moment. Everything became very sharp: the feel of my costume, the smell of the theater, my vision. Our cue came and off we went. The scene was fine. Hey, I thought, if it is okay to feel whatever I feel, I can do this for a long time! And I did. I began to relax and enjoy the run for over a year. I let myself feel whatever I felt as I acted.

This technique of being in my body has saved me through many challenging acting experiences.

When I started teaching acting, it soon became evident that one of my principle jobs was to help my students get present. Otherwise, their acting would be stiff, forced, wooden, and lacking in aliveness. Quickly I discovered one simple question that I ask my students right before they are about to perform (either acting or singing). It is the question that leads them into their bodies and into their characters. I give it to you. It is simply:

WHAT ARE YOU EXPERIENCING IN YOUR BODY RIGHT NOW?

That simple question is one of the most powerful questions you can ask yourself. *All* the information you need about your character is in your body if you are willing to be listen to it. The body is your source for information and creativity. The truth is, once you step into a character, you will begin to feel what that character feels whether you know it or not. Better to consciously know it. Bringing your character's feelings and thoughts into your life without consciously knowing what you are doing can be disastrous.

In an early class a young woman did a Shakespearean monologue. It was the worst kind of "stock" acting. Afterward, I said to her gently, "Let's do it again, but before you start, tell me what you are experiencing in your body right now."

She said, "Actually, my stomach hurts. I was finding it hard to do the monologue because of it."

"Where does it hurt?"

"Right in the pit of my stomach."

(Notice that all my questions are merely to increase her consciousness.)

"What does it feel like right in the pit of your stomach?"

"It's a burning sensation."

"Can you let it be there, and let it be as intense as it wants to be?" (In other words, I was encouraging her not to suppress the sensation.)

"Yes. It's like a fire right now. Flames."

"Good. Do you feel present with it?"

"Yes."

"Just do the monologue and express the fire in your stomach."

She did, and her performance blew us away, as they say. Afterwards, she began to cry. She knew that she had gone from zero to sixty in her acting and surprised—even stunned herself. "How did I do that?" She wailed. "And how do I do that again?"

Already, as all of us tend to do, she was thinking about the future. I said to her, "You can do that and even better as you are more and more willing to be present."

It was the experience with that young woman that prompted me to name my two-day workshop for actors and singers *The Creative Explosion* because it doesn't actually have to take years to be brilliant if one is courageous enough and conscious enough to Be Present in the body and start from there. It does take courage, because to be fully present in your body means letting go of controlling what you feel. That is not to say letting go of control, but letting go of controlling—an important distinction. The mind is dedicated and well-trained to do whatever it can to control our feelings, change them, and even deny them. We have all been so over-programmed regarding our

30

sensations that most of us have become cut off from our bodies.

Being present means to feel what you feel, not what you think you should feel. So often—more often than not—actors or singers will get present in their bodies and then declare that what they are feeling is *wrong*. But if you will allow yourself to be present in your body, you will find out information about your character that is far more interesting than anything you can think up. It may even be contrary to what you were thinking about that character.

When you are present, you are not acting out some preconceived idea of the character that is akin to painting by the numbers.

The last scene of a play I was in was a highly dramatic one, but opening night as I approached the door to enter, I found myself exhausted. All I wanted to do was go home and go to bed. For a moment I worried about my exhaustion given I knew that the scene I was walking into was a highly dramatic one. Fortunately I quickly realized that my character had been out most of the night walking and probably all *she* wanted to do was go home and go to bed. Besides, she had no idea there was a dramatic scene waiting for her on the other side of the door, so I let go of worrying or trying to change what I felt and the scene went very well.

When you are present, you are not ahead of yourself—not even for a second. When you are present, you are spontaneously responding to the moment.

Try on the possibility that everything you feel is what the character is feeling. Everything you think is what the character is thinking. There is no preparation more valuable than this simple focus on exactly what you are feeling just before you perform.

Being Present leads to wonderful information and surprises. Learning to trust where you are (rather than trying to be where you think you should be) will open up your creativity to a level you cannot imagine. It takes daring. It takes courage to simply be where you are. But once you have experienced what happens when you dare to let go and be, you will never want to go back to trying to make yourself be where you aren't.

At first, actors who have been trained in other acting techniques find Being Present startling, sometimes alarming, but ultimately relieving, because Being Present eliminates the stress of self-manipulation and struggling to "feel" something. It simply does not matter what you feel before you perform. Truly it doesn't. If you are willing to be exactly where you are and start from there, you will find yourself carried along by your role rather than trying to shove it along or force it to be what you have decided it should be.

Animals and children are naturally present. An old show biz axiom cautions actors not to get on stage with a dog because a dog is so present it will steal the scene, unless, and this is possible, the actor is just as present. (See Tom Hanks in *Turner and Hooch*.)

Animals can act, too. Ducks pretend to have broken wings to lure predators away from the nest. A mother duck is really convincing as she flops and struggles, but once the predator far enough away from the nest, watch her suddenly recover and take flight. Acting is as natural as having sex (although it tends to get just as complicated.) In order to be authentic in acting, you have to remove the restrictions your training has put on you. You have to learn again how to be as present as a child, a dog, or a duck.

However, learning how to be present is the one principle actors resist the most, because it means letting go of protective covers. It means becoming vulnerable, feeling, and opening the heart. That's not easy. We have all been trained to think rather than be. Thinking puts us and the world in safe, little boxes. Being blasts those boxes apart. Not only are we trained to think, we *want* to stay in thought because it is where our sense of control is, false though it may be.

If you now understand that Being Present is one of the All Important Keys to Acting, tattoo this simple question somewhere in your mind, and before you perform, ask yourself:

WHAT SENSATION AM I EXPERIENCING IN MY BODY RIGHT NOW?

Then, pour all of what you are feeling and thinking into your character. Simon Callow is right. Sensation is at the heart of acting. Notice that the question is *NOT*, "What are you feeling right now?" Or "What are you thinking?" The question is, "What sensation are you experiencing in your body right now?" This question sometimes leads to intensified emotions and highly creative and informative images.

"What's going on in your body?" is not a question we are asked normally. Usually, we are asked what we think or what we feel about something. So, learning to answer that question often takes actors some time and practice. Initially, actors may respond with something like, "I feel stupid," which is not a feeling at all but a thought. Or an actor might say, "I feel nervous." which is a generalized feeling but closer to being present and leads to a more specific inquiry, "*Where* in your body do you feel nervous?" When the actor starts to describe the particular sensations attached to the feeling of nervousness (for one person it is cold hands, for another sweating palms, etc.), he is becoming consciously present.

Being present in your body will give you all the information you need about your character. Think of starting from where you are as your springboard into the monologue or scene. Get present, add or subtract nothing and start from there.

Almost as important as Getting Present as your jumping off place is consciously Getting Present after your have performed. I call it "Landing."

LANDING

Landing after a performance is vital. Before you start and after you finish are critical times in performing. It's like flying a plane. You have to take off and you have to land. Both must be done carefully and consciously. The problem with acting and singing is that the characters, the play, the song is still with us after the words stop and the curtain comes down. If you don't know this, you will believe that what you are thinking and feeling is about you and not about the character. An important key to remember is that: *How you land is not how you did.*

A character may fail in the play or the scene, but an actor who doesn't *land consciously* may mistakenly think *he* has failed. It's dangerous for an actor not to take the time to land with the character.

I have fallen into that error so many times, I urge you to learn this now. In the first few plays I was in I fell madly in love with my leading men. After the ends of the run, somehow, I wasn't in love with them any more. After about the fifth time I made a vow not to get into a relationship with my on stage love interests. (I have almost always kept that vow.)

Even with all my experience in giving my feelings and thoughts to the character rather than taking them on personally, after the first performance of *Laughing Wild*, I felt such humiliation that I ran into my dressing room and hid behind some hanging clothes thinking, "Oh, god, the audience *HATED* ME!" (Remember my character had been in and out of mental hospitals.) The director and Christopher Durang came bopping happily into my room and were startled when they saw me cowering and crying. "What's wrong?!" they looked at me horrified.

"I was awful! The audience hated me!"

My first clue that maybe I was incorrect was seeing them look at one another as if I was crazy (which I was). Taking me by the hand, they ushered me out for a reassuring drink and talk during which I realized what had happened: I was still in my character. And without going into a great deal of detail, my upset had taught me something important about the character that I had not realized. Having gotten the information, I never felt that way again after a performance of that play.

I did a play about a psychiatrist who went to Bosnia to try to help survivors. At the end of the first performance, I went back to my dressing room, gripped the dressing table and thought, "I've got to quit acting. It's too hard."

"Wait a minute," my Wiser Self said. "Is this how your character feels?"

"Of course!" I realized. In the play my character came home and decided not to be a psychiatrist any more. She quit because she felt that she had failed, and that being a psychiatrist was too hard. I looked in the mirror, smiled, and relaxed. I didn't have to give up acting just because my character gave up being a psychiatrist.

Landing is not only important for your sanity as an actor, it gives you information about the character that you may not have known beforehand. In fact, everything you need to know about a character, you will discover through being present before and after you work.

At the end of one scene in class an actor said, "I didn't do the scene well. I feel really defeated."

"Does your character feel defeated?" I ask the actor.

He looks at me surprised. "Oh! Yeah!"

"Give it to the character," I remind him. He does, and he comes out of the emotional tunnel he was digging for himself. Actors in my classes learn that for a time after the monologue, scene, or song, the character still reverberates in them emotionally. So even after the scene is over and you're driving home, give everything you think and feel to your character. It could continue to reverberate for a day or so. Be alert. Be conscious. And welcome the information you're getting about the character—probably it's something that you hadn't quite realized.

Give everything you think and feel to your character.

If you can learn to give absolutely everything you think and feel to your character, you will save yourself so much personal sturm und drang. Even the most experienced actors can fall into the quagmire of taking on their character's difficulties thinking it's about them personally. Recently, I performed in a play with a brilliant 87 year-old, very experienced actor, who came off stage looking distraught. He whispered to me, "Oh, god, I did a terrible job." He actually had been quite brilliant. I took him by the arms and said, "That's your character still talking. Tell me. Doesn't he believe that he did a terrible job?" After a moment, his eyes brightened a bit. "Oh, yeah. Yeah, he does! But I had trouble remembering my lines!"

"Isn't that the main plight of your character? He's starting to forget things?" I asked him.

"Oh, yeah! Yes, it is!" Then, he smiled, and I shook him playfully. "You are such a good actor you don't even know you're still him!" We laughed, but it was true. This man is a brilliant actor. The better you are as an actor, the more likely you are going to walk off stage still being that character. Let yourself land afterwards! Do not turn that character into you. Learn to land consciously, so you can get the information you need and let it go.

Acting and singing are not nine to five jobs. We don't just walk away when we are in the middle of creating a character or story. It is with us all the time. And that can be fun or hell. When we aren't actually rehearsing or writing, we still must give everything that we feel and think—every reaction we have to everything that happens to us in a day—to our characters. We must know how to be present with it all but not take it personally. A student of mine called while she was in the middle of doing a play. "It's awful," she wails. "For some reason, everyone in the cast seems to be against me and snubs me."

"Is this how their characters treat your character?" I ask.

Small pause.

"Uh. Yeah. Absolutely."

"Don't take it personally. Give how you feel about it to your character."

In an interesting parallel to the idea that children feel what the parents don't feel, you will feel whatever your character does NOT feel. What affects us most as actors and writers is not necessarily what the character expresses, it's what the character doesn't express or is hidden. So it is important to know how aware and how present your character is. Does your character have addictions? Are they not facing their own feelings? What are they addicted to? How are they avoiding their own feelings?

Years ago I was a heavy smoker. I was in a company directed by the indomitable June Havoc. This was a woman of great courage who had lived through and triumphed over many adversities and carved out one of the longest careers in show business. She was a powerhouse of a woman, so I listened to her.

One day she said to me in her deep, theatrical voice, "Katherine! Your body is your temple! Stop smoking!" So I did. That released all the rage and power and fire in me that had gone up in cigarette smoke. I pass this on to you. "Your body is your temple. Stop smoking! Stop all your addictions!" The only purpose of addictions is to suppress or change sensations and emotions that you cannot bear to feel. Stopping your addictions is a wildly effective method for becoming more present in your body—uncomfortable, but powerful.

One reason we love artists and actors is because they are present (at least when they're acting). They go where we fear to go and take us with them, giving us, the audience, the safety to feel things we cannot feel when we are alone with ourselves. Actors are at the vanguard of feeling and sensation.

The fact that Being Present is simple does not mean it is easy. In fact, it is very hard. It requires mastery but not control. It requires bravery. Really being in your body and allowing yourself to be seen is an intimacy (into-me-see) that makes you feel very exposed and vulnerable. But that is necessary for brilliant, authentic acting. To be present means to feel everything. As an actor and creator, you must be able to stand in the presence of all human experience. It's your job. Human sensations and emotions are the colors on the palette you use to paint your pictures. If you resist a sensation, you will not have that color available to paint with. Therefore, you must be able to feel all feelings and *sensations* surrounding love, hate, anger, boredom, sexual arousal, fear, terror, vulnerability, trust, willingness, courage, volatility, rage, weakness, strength, determination, apathy, death, physical pain, cowardice, fragility, and every other human experience.

Learning how to Be Present, not just in acting but in life, is one of the keystones of my *Creative Explosion* workshops. In my book, *The Four Principles: Applying the Four Keys of Authentic Acting to Life,* there is a chapter on how to partner with someone called The Getting Present Process. It is a powerful, life-changing experience if practiced on a regular basis. It has completely expanded my life as well as the lives of many others. Given that the process was bestowed on me by the angels or the gods, I feel no ownership over it. It is a process that will help you to Be Here Now in a way you never imagined.

Even without this specific process, learn not to run from the sensations of fear and terror, go into them. Go into your sadness and grief. Don't run from any sensation that you find uncomfortable whatever it might be: cold, tightness in the throat, pounding heart, adrenaline rush, heat, numbness, fatigue. Screw up your courage and dive into your body. When you can stand in the presence of any sensation, you will have mastered this all important key to brilliant and authentic acting.

RELAXATION

Relaxation is the secret of all good acting.
--John Gielgud, *Early Stages*

Unless on *accepts* whatever sensations that arise in the body, one is not relaxed. Acceptance is the foremost hallmark of Relaxation. And Relaxation is the hallmark of a great actor. Not without justification did John Gielgud believe that Relaxation is the be all and end all of good acting. It is the one discernable difference between the experienced actor and the novice. Beginning actors often work too hard at acting, as if they believe that tension and effort is what good acting is all about. Paradoxically, the more relaxed an actor is the deeper and fuller their emotions will be without any straining for them.

How important is Relaxation to acting and creativity? Without it, expression becomes constipated, stopped, and stuck—veering towards turmoil and struggle. In order to create and keep creating, one must aim for Relaxation. It is a vital key to brilliant acting.

The characteristics of Relaxation are: willingness, acceptance, ease, lightness, surrender, humor, self-confidence, playfulness, embracing, trust, and faith. The opposite of Relaxation is heaviness, weightiness, seriousness, resistance, significance, rigidity, negative thinking, holding on, willfulness, worry, tension, gravity.

Where does Relaxation come from?

While Being Present is all about the body, Relaxation *is all about the mind*. Relaxation, or lack of Relaxation, comes from thought. As we learn to unfetter the body, we must learn to discipline the mind and not allow it to run roughshod over our creativity and prevent us from creating. I don't know if it is possible to be completely relaxed without some form of spirituality. Start with willingness, graduate to acceptance and then, if you can climb all the way up to the heady heights of trust and faith, you will have achieved the ultimate of Relaxation and, perhaps, spiritual enlightenment.

When actors understand how important Relaxation is, they often seek out any technique such as yoga and meditation that will increase their higher awareness and consciousness. However, in training the mind to choose the contexts of Relaxation, do not to use any technique to by-pass Being Present. Do not use the mind not to feel. Do not fall into the "enlightenment trap" which is knowing and saying all the right things but acting and feeling something else entirely.

Being present and accepting where you are is not easy. It requires an ongoing personal mastery. The actors, writers, and directors who can do that have long, valuable careers. Too often, in an effort to stop uncomfortable sensations and to calm their minds, creative people fall prey to addictions. There are too many examples of talented stars who died young from addictions.

What is Relaxation in acting?

Relaxation is essentially ***accepting*** what you are feeling in your body and giving it to the character. If you can accept great emotions like terror and grief and rage and uncomfortable sensations like tension, numbness, tiredness, apathy, or sleepiness and give them to the

40

character, you have mastered relaxation in acting, and dare I say, life.

Relaxation is not about lack of energy, or is it necessarily about feeling good and calm. The moment you start fighting what you feel or resisting it in any way, you lose Relaxation. Because of this, I call Relaxation "The-last-to-get-the-first-to-go" principle. A soupçon of unaccepted emotion destroys Relaxation like a drop of ink clouds a clear glass of water.

It's almost impossible to talk about Relaxation without addressing Being Present. What we feel may even contradict what we *think* a character should think or feel. Sometimes actors will emphatically state that what they are feeling is *wrong!* But if they park their judgment and express what they truly feel, the result is wondrously inspired. In one of my workshops, an actress got present before doing a comic monologue. She felt very sad and started to cry. I told her to begin from there, but her *mind* said that she shouldn't feel sad. "It's all wrong!" she wailed. "I'm not supposed to be sad! This is a comic monologue!"

"Well, be wrong," I said. "Blubber through it. Let's see what happens." So, eyes streaming, nose running, she did the monologue, and it was hilarious. We all screamed with laughter. Afterwards, she understood how appropriate the sadness was for the comedy in the monologue. The information came from her body—even in opposition to her mind.

A student was about to perform a monologue from *Medea.*. Medea is very angry at her husband, right? That's why she kills her children, yes? She's really angry—really mad at Jason. Yet, when the actress got up to perform, what she felt was terror—stark, raving terror. Her mind told her this is not what Medea should be feeling, but I asked her to just express from this terror. She was trembling. She began and delivered one of the most stunning and terrifying performances of Medea I could

41

imagine. Her emotions were so intense that it was clear that underneath that kind of rage *is* terror. Her performance stunned and surprised us all—including her. When the mind is aligned with the body rather than trying to control it, the collaboration is brilliant.

Relaxation means letting go of trying. I was in rehearsal for a filming of a Horton Foote short play. The director kept asking me for "more energy." I kept pushing myself, and he was still not satisfied. On the day of the filming, which took place in a house, I was standing in front of a screen door while the makeup man and the hair person were getting me ready. It was a lovely fall day. I could hear a leaf blower in the distance: leaves were gently drifting to the ground. It was a blissful moment. "Oh, the hell with it," I thought. "Let him fire me. I'm just going to do it from this simple joy."

At the end of the scene, the director shouted from the other room, "That's what I was talking about!" My energy came from being present and accepting where I was. I didn't think my joy fit the character, but evidently, it did. From then on I knew that when a director asked for more energy, I needed to stop fighting myself.

Give up trying. Don't even say the word "trying." "Try" is the word hypnotists use when they *don't* want someone to do something. "Try to open your eyes! You can't!" Try means to struggle.

Terrible difficulties and problems in acting come from not being consciously present. An unconscious actor can end up *acting out* the character rather than *being* it, creating chaos around himself and everyone else. A good rule of thumb is: *Give everything that you think and feel to the character.* Even a very experienced professional actor will be drawn into the thought that what he is feeling is about **him**. How many times has the following happened in Hollywood? Actors fall in love with their fellow actors during filming, end their marriages and a few months later wonder what they saw in the other person and end that relationship.

There was an old movie about an actor who, while playing Othello, lost control and killed the actress playing Desdemona. Hopefully, nothing like that has ever happened in real life, but I have seen many an actor crash on the shoals of not knowing that what they were feeling belonged to the character. It is much, much better to be aware of this natural, organic, creative phenomenon, and use it consciously.

Not only are you going to experience everything the character feels, you are also going to experience everything that your character *doesn't* feel. This is where it can get very tricky. It is important to know what devices the character uses in order not to feel. Is your character afflicted with negative judgment, addiction, conflict, lying, doubt, procrastination, perfectionism, denial, righteousness, cynicism, obsession, or any other negative mindset? Underneath all these devices are unfelt feelings.

I have found easier to play a character who is expressive of her feelings (i.e. Rosalind in *As You Like It*) than to play one who is not (i.e. the mean, high society Mrs. Parmour in the BBC's *Buccaneers*). When you land after playing unexpressed characters, their unfelt feelings will arise in you. Emotions that characters don't express and may not even know they feel will come gushing up. Because of this, it is vital that you land and give what you are feeling to the character without taking these feelings on and thinking they are about you. Be conscious of what happens after the play is over.

You must learn to relax in life as an actor. Accept that fear, disappointment, and bad reviews are just part of the job description. Do your best not to read reviews—even the good ones. Shirley Knight once told me that she never read reviews because "Even when they're good, they're never good enough." You will be afraid. Stand in your fear and let it burn out. Do not allow your mind to say things like, "I suck." "That was awful." "I'm not good enough, thin enough, pretty enough, strong enough, handsome enough, talented enough, blah, blah, blah." All negative thoughts about yourself and what you are doing are just your mind's attempt to get you to stop expressing yourself creatively. Your poor mind, like an over-anxious parent, is trying to protect you from doing anything that is going to frighten IT.

Understand that fear is just your mind telling you it's not going to work out. Train yourself to believe that it will work out. Do not believe your mind when it tries to stop you. "You're going to fail! Don't sing! Don't act!" Instead of fighting negative thoughts, put your attention on what you are feeling and let your emotions be like weather. Are you raining sadness? Put up the umbrella of compassion and let it rain. Don't even ask if you're talented enough. You are. Now, do it.

Achieving Relaxation is not easy. Training the mind is hard and demands as much daily attention as Being Present, Being Committed and Communication do.

Once you have learned to handle your negative mind, you are free to express yourself and take risks.

Use your mind to create the context for Relaxation so that you can stay in touch with your love and joy of acting. Look at failure as a teacher. Start retraining your mind to see the future positively rather than as something fearful.

Remember, we call it a play or a screenplay.

COMMUNICATE

"You walk into the room, you look the guy in the eye and you tell the truth."

--James Cagney

Once you are present, relaxed, and committed, the only thing to do is Communicate. Some actors believe communication is the key—the only key to acting. One can argue for that, although one can also make the same claim for all the other keys as well. Communication is what I call the Fail Safe Key. Communication will save you. If you don't know your Commitment, don't feel present, and can't relax, Communication will open your parachute when you're falling and don't know where the rip cord is.

When I did the movie *Suspect*, it was an extremely challenging situation that I wrote about at length in my other book, *The Four Principles:Applying the Keys of Brilliant Acting to Life.*. What saved me was communicating with Dennis Quaid. Before I made my entrance in my first scene, I was convinced the director wanted to fire me. However, I was present, went through the open doors and the crowd of extras and found my marks to begin the scene with Dennis. It was like finding a life raft in a stormy sea. He is a great communicator. I grabbed on. We did the scene in one take. The director was very chatty afterward, which was a complete transformation from his behavior towards me before the shot. The rest of our scenes were done in one take, which I attribute largely to Dennis Quaid.

Every great actor and great director I have been lucky enough to work with are generous communicators. Give yourself to the other people you work with. Give yourself to the audience. Be generous with your communication, and you can never go wrong in acting.

Communicating is a two-way street. It's not only speaking but listening. Some actors will go so far as to say that acting is all about listening—that acting is really reacting. Communicating is not just listening with your ears, it is listening with your eyes. It is absorbing through the eyes both what the other person is saying and their reaction to what you are saying.

The eyes are so important in communication. Lovers look deeply into one another's eyes. Enemies do as well. Since all of drama is about love or its opposite, actors must learn to look into someone's eyes without looking away. One of the first things I need to do with some students is ask them to look in the other person's eyes. This often makes them uncomfortable because it forces them to feel. Most people don't want their feelings to be seen, so they have learned to look away from another person when they start to experience some sensation. This is because communicating will intensify feelings, which, of course, is a good thing in acting. Practice communicating without looking away. It will be very uncomfortable if you're not used to it, but you will seem more and be more confident as a result.

Great actors are what I call Laser Communicators. They look right at you, and their eyes pierce right into your soul. If you want to be a really good actor, be brave. Laser Communicate. Not communicating should be a conscious choice in acting. Not communicating is an indication that you want to hide something or hide from someone.

Just as lack of relaxation stops movement, so does non-communication. It creates a wall that cannot be penetrated. Cutting off communication is a disempowerment. It is the last resort of the rebellious teenager and the prisoner. "I only have to tell you my name, rank, and serial number!" Heroes in films are tortured in an effort to force them to communicate and spill the beans. The first thing an army does is try to destroy the enemy's ability to communicate. Once the enemy's communication is cut off, they have all but lost. This is the power of non-communication.

Non-communication also conveys shyness and lack of confidence. If you want to appear in charge, look the guy in the eye and tell the truth, like Cagney says. When actors do not communicate to one another, an audience will not understand what they are trying to say. Many times in my acting classes, if actors in scenes do not communicate, I ask them to do it again not looking away from their partner. This can be difficult for them, but the feedback from the class always includes comments like "I understood the scene better" or "I heard things I didn't hear the first time." It doesn't take long for my students to understand the power of Laser Communication.

Great actors and great writers are simply great communicators. Shakespeare is The Ultimate Great Communicator because he digs deep into human experience and puts all of it, every nuance, every subtlety, every painful experience into words. However, if an actor in a Shakespeare play is trying to "act" rather than communicate, then Shakespeare seems out-dated, boring and befuddling.

At the simplest level, our communication must be heard. I recently saw a singer/composer perform at a benefit. He put his head back, closed his eyes and mumbled the words to his song. It was as if he didn't care if we, the audience, understood him. And we didn't. As his songs progressed, we looked around the table at one another in dismay. At one point we all heard one word "bible" and were so delighted we bandied it back and forth for the rest of the night.

I was once fortunate enough to be cast as Toby Landau in a tour of Neil Simon's *Gingerbread Lady* starring the inimitable Maureen Stapleton. One night we were to appear in a tent. There happened to be a torrential rain that thundered on the canvas like a drum. As Maureen and I stood at the back waiting to go on, we couldn't hear a word the actors were saying. There were three microphones hanging above the stage area. They didn't seem to help. Maureen said to me. "Head for one of the microphones and shout into it." We went on. I did as she said. I headed for it and yelled my long monologue into the microphone, forgetting the blocking and "acting." At the end of it, the audience rose to their feet with applause—not for my acting. They were just so grateful to hear the play. No one will know whether you're brilliant or not if they don't hear you. Speak out.

Communication is physical as well as verbal. Every thing we do on stage is a kind of communication. An audience is amazingly perceptive and alert to the smallest gesture and the tiniest movement. One time I saw a show at Radio City Music hall. In a line up of some fifty Rockettes all dressed alike, standing at a curtain call, one of them blew out her lips softly with fatigue. It was a small gesture but so real, and it was one of the funniest moments I have ever seen on stage. It communicated "I'm exhausted" vividly and truthfully. When it is real, the smallest movement will communicate profoundly.

Communication is energetic. When an actor is hit by an emotion, a real and unexpected emotion, we, in the audience, feel it at the same time. The actor may have done very little, a mere stoppage of the breath, but we can feel it across space—even a lot of space—way back in the balcony. We will be hit in the heart at the same instant the actor is. The actor can have his or her back to us and we will still feel it.

We must always communicate to someone or something. Non-communication is symptomatic of insanity. If you want to look crazy, don't communicate. One time an actor brought in a monologue to class. He didn't communicate to anyone. I thought maybe the character was crazy. He certainly looked nuts. And I didn't really understand what he was saying. Afterwards, I asked him to do it again looking someone right in the eye. The difference was startling. Suddenly, I understood what he was saying, and he didn't seem crazy any more.

Often in a play or film, a character tells a story about something that happened in the past. Sometimes an actor will stop communicating to the other actor while telling the story and go into a kind of reverie mode. Try not to do this. The story is not about the past. The story is about now. The character is telling that story to that particular person *for a reason*. Don't disappear into the past with a story about the past. Tell it now for a reason that has to do with now. It's a confession. It's an opening up to that person. It's justifying yourself to that person. It's not just about isolating and reliving the past, no matter how vivid the story may be. Communicate now.

When you communicate to an audience enroll them into relationship with you by rewarding response. Your acting partner is the audience. Years ago, I saw Pauline Collins do *Shirley Valentine*. It's a one-woman show. She made the audience fall in love with her in 15 seconds by rewarding response. She said a line and a man coughed— not even in response to what she said, but she looked in his direction and delivered the next line. She won the audience in that instant. What she communicated was "I know you're there, and you know I know you're there and I'm going to talk directly to you and register your responses." All that in one second. The audience loved

49

her for that. As an audience, it's wonderful to be known and responded to. It's part of the magic of theater. It's an energetic exchange that exists nowhere else. It's why film actors love to do theater. It's why theater will never die. It is an exhilarting experience to be in this energy of communication.

Be clear about what you are communicating. What is the response you want from your listener or listeners? A friend of mine had her purse stolen on the street. She was furious. "He stole my purse!" She started screaming her rage. People around her were too startled to take action. They were looking at her rather than at the man running. She realized later that she had been more invested in expressing her outrage than in getting her purse back.

An actress in my class did a scene in which she was talking to a committee. She was very emotional and angry. I asked her afterward, "What response do you want from the committee? What do you really want and need from them?"

"I want them to do something about the situation—change their vote."

"Then do the scene again and communicate in a way to get them to do that." She did it again. She was not so emotional because she was more invested in convincing them. Be very clear about what the character *really* wants and is trying to communicate. Communicate your energy out rather than going inward. Do your best to try to achieve what it is that your character really wants through Laser, generous, and clear communication.

And, remember, if you aren't really clear about what your character needs and wants, Communicate. It is the Fail Safe Principle. It will help you *find* the other keys if you don't know where they are or have lost them.

MYSTERY

"It's a mystery!"
--from the film *Shakespeare in Love*

Mystery is not the fifth key. It is what we step into when all the Four Keys are fulfilled. Mystery is what surrounds the keys. It glues them together. It is at the core of each one.

A great performance, a great piece of writing, seems to come from a force that cannot be defined. Many great artists claim they are not the creators of their work—that the writing or acting flows through them from some unknown source. Great, classic songs have been written in a half an hour. Performances often sweep away the performer. Ideas and songs and inspiration seem to come from nowhere. Where does this creativity come from?

Sometimes our creations look as if they are never going to be realized—never come together—and then, they do. When asked how such a great performance could come about after such a disastrous dress rehearsal, Geoffrey Rush, playing the producer in *Shakespeare in Love*, smiled, shrugged his shoulders and responded, "It's a mystery."

A famous story about Laurence Olivier illustrates this leap into the unfathomable. One night his performance in *Othello* went beyond anything anyone had ever seen. The ovations were thunderous. The other actors were awed. Afterwards, Olivier stomped to his dressing room and slammed the door shut, obviously in a kind of fury. A friend ventured in. "What's wrong, Larry?! Why are you upset? That was the most brilliant performance of your life."

"I know!" Olivier growled. "And I don't know how I did it!"

Great artists rarely attempt or succeed in defining their own creations or process. Indeed, this experience of being taken by some mysterious creative force is well known to anyone who creates. It is sought after but cannot be summoned. When it happens, it is as if one takes that quantum leap from a Newtonian Universe into a wild Einsteinian one. I have been lucky to witness so many of these magical performances. Being on stage with the extraordinary Maureen Stapleton in *Gingerbread Lady* was one such time. She was so wonderful one could not imagine anyone else in the role. She had a secret relationship with that character that defied definition. Her characterization fulfilled all the Four Keys so organically, that her performance was lifted into the sublime. Yet she could not articulate it herself. When I asked her for advice on acting, she said, "Fast is good. Faster is better."

Anthony Hopkins came to a period in his career when he felt uninspired. He decided he was bored with analyzing characters as he had done. Instead, he decided to learn his lines "cold" before rehearsal, so he could be free to allow himself to follow his impulses. His career took on new life via his terrifying and inspired turn as Hannibal Lecter in *The Silence of the Lambs*.

To see Vanessa Redgrave's last few minutes on screen in the film *Atonement* is to see an actress at the height of her powers. She is so raw and real, so completely relaxed, so heartfelt, one can see her soul in her eyes. She hides nothing and disguises nothing. I was so swept away by her performance that I replayed the scene several times, and then replayed it again with the director's remarks. At her entrance, the director whispered reverently, "There's God." Ah, yes.

Jesus and The Lost Goddess by Timothy Freke & Peter Gandy begins with the statement "Life is a mystery. A mystery so awesome that we insulate ourselves from its intensity." Yes. Music up. Nelson Eddy and Jeannette MacDonald sing thrillingly, "Ah, Sweet Mystery of life at last I've found you! Ah, 'tis love and love alone....."

When commitment comes from the deepest love, it opens us up to awe. When we are fully present we step into a realm of *I am* that feels as if we are God or close to God. When we are in a state of surrender and peace, this deep relaxation is blissful and puts us close to the Mystery of it all. When we connect with others profoundly, we touch on the Oneness of Life that poets and priests know well.

There are no techniques or exercises that will lead you directly to a realization of the magical in creativity. We all yearn to be swept along in its current. And most of us have had at some moment that delicious experience—of being in its flow. Experience and time can, hopefully, lead us as actors to achieve such a high level of mastery that we are truly open to it, willing, and ready without force or resistance.

When you are deeply committed, intensely present, masterfully relaxed and in powerful communication, your creativity *will* take that quantum leap into magical realms beyond your wildest dreams. Fulfilling the Four Keys, however, will require you to be brave and take creative risks with abandon and trust. Have courage, step forward, and leap trusting you will soar into the land of Mystery.

Which brings me to a cautionary warning: protect your love for acting. If you don't love your role, or cannot find

53

a way to love and enjoy what you are doing, that will cause you to suffer. As an actor, going against yourself, betraying your creative self, will damage and even destroy the love with which you began your career. And when you lose your love and your ability to commit, you have lost your creative spirit. Your love, therefore, is a kind of sacred space you must hold for yourself.

Do not let any teacher, director, or person harm that love any more than you would allow someone to abuse, harm, or neglect someone you deeply love. Your creative self *is* your inner child. Protect it. Listen to it. Guide it. Allow it. Validate it. Never criticize it. Do not sell yourself down the river creatively.

Acting is not about getting saved. Do not use that love to try to get the love you never had in your life. Hold your creative self close and safe to your heart. Expressing your creative inner child requires you to be vulnerable. Do not under any circumstances give away your power to any authority. At the same time, learn from those in authority positions. Listen to them and collaborate without sacrificing yourself in any way. That does not mean to be argumentative or uncooperative. In fact, doing that is allowing your child to rule. You, the wise, adult part must guide, care for, and empower your inner creative child so that your inner child can express. Find the love, protect the love, be true to that love, strengthen that love and you will find your way through all the rejections, difficulties, stressful situations, and problems of being an actor.

It's a glorious life. There can be nothing more enlightening than the life of an actor. Have fun. Open your heart knowing you can and will protect it. When you express yourself freely, you will love yourself, everyone, and the world.

A Tribute to June Havoc

June scared me when I first saw her. Hollywood glamorous, she had blond hair, a perfect dancer body, and a low, thrilling voice. I felt like a hick next her and was overwhelmed by her energy and powerful presence.

She had come to Atlanta, GA to the Alliance Theater to direct her fascinating play, *Marathon 33*. I had been cast sight-unseen in a supporting role as Rita Marimba. I assumed she would be a lousy director. I fled to Michael Howard, the artistic director. "Get me out of this show!" I begged. "She's all gold lamé! She'll roll right over me!"

"She's wonderful. Just go to one day of rehearsal." He waved me away.

So I went and was soon converted by her genius. I looked up her history. Starting at the age of two as Dainty Baby June, she toe-danced her way to stardom in vaudeville. When she outgrew daintiness, her mother, Rose, shoved her aside and put all her attention on sister Louise, transforming her into Gypsy Rose Lee. At age 14, June, alone in the world, entered Marathon Dances just to be able to eat. She made her way to New York, a starring role in *Pal Joey*, and a long and active career in show biz.

Later, I happily joined June's repertory company in New Orleans. Tragically, Gypsy had just died of lung cancer from smoking. June never gave up hounding me to quit. So I did. Given that my own sister, a smoker, died of lung cancer, I believe I am alive today because of June.

I not only owe June my life but so much of what has been good in it. She cast me as Blanche DuBois and directed a stunning production of *Streetcar* right there in New Orleans. It was one of the great experiences of my career. She also took care of two stray dogs I had found until I could buy a house which she also found for me.

She was a mother, a mentor, a model of strength and courage to me. I will forever be grateful, and I will never forget her. Thank you, June, from the bottom of my heart.

www.ingramcontent.com/pod-product-compliance
Lightning Source LLC
Chambersburg PA
CBHW021226020426
42331CB00003B/484